EXTRAORDINARY

DUETS

24 CONTEMPORARY AND INSPIRATIONAL SONGS

DUETS

ARRANGED BY
TOM FETTKE

Donna Brier

CONTENTS

We Trust in the Name of the Lord Our God

Words and Music by
STEVEN CURTIS CHAPMAN
Arranged by Camp Kirkland
Duet arrangement by Tom Fettke

We trust in the name of the Lord our God. His love nev - er fails, His

Cued notes optional

name will al - ways pre - vail; We trust in the name of the Lord.

We trust in the name of the Lord. We trust in the name of the Lord our

God, our God.

The Great Divide

Words and Music by
GRANT CUNNINGHAM
and MATT HUESMAN
Arranged by Dennis Allen
Duet arrangement by Tom Fettke

1. Si - lence, tryin' to fath-om the dis - tance, Look-in' out cross the can - yon carved by
   faith - ful, on my own I'm un - a - ble. He found me hope-less, a - lone, and sent a

   my — hands. God is gra - cious. Sin would still sep-a-rate us Were it not for the
   Sav - ior. He's pro-vid - ed a path and prom-ised to guide us Safe-ly past all the

Though Your Sins Be As Scarlet

with
Wonderworking Power

Words and Music by
WAYNE GOODINE
Arranged by Tom Fettke

It mat-ters not where you have been,

It mat-ters not what you have done.

There is cleans-ing from

ev-ery sin, In the blood of God's own Son, God's own

Son.

18

Think About His Love

Words and Music by
WALT HARRAH
Arranged by Tom Fettke

Out of His Great Love

Words and Music by
TERRY and BARBI FRANKLIN
Arranged by Tom Fettke and Kyle Hill

With energy ♩ = ca. 140

Out of His great love He picked me up,

Set my feet on a stur- dy rock; Out of His great love I've learned the

(to pg. 25, ms. 8)

1

mean - ing ___ of Sal - va - tion out of His great love. Out of

A♭   E♭/G   A♭   E♭/B♭   B♭7   E♭   A♭/B♭

2   *Low voice solo* (17)

love.   *mf* I had gone a - stray, I had lost my way When I

E♭   B♭/D   Cm   B♭/D   E♭   A♭

(21)

called up - on His name; Then He res - cued me, now the

A♭   B♭   E♭   E♭/G   A♭   B♭   A♭/B♭

song I sing: ___

E♭   E♭/G   A♭

28

In the Presence of Jehovah

Words and Music by
GERON DAVIS
Arranged by Marty Parks
Duet arrangement by Tom Fettke

Here I Am, Lord

Words and Music by
DANIEL L. SCHUTTE
Arranged by Marty Parks
Duet arrangement by Tom Fettke

40

It Was Enough

Words and Music by
LARRY BRYANT
Arranged by Camp Kirkland
Duet arrangement by Tom Fettke

44

Joy of My Desire

Words and Music by
JENNIFER RANDOLPH
Arranged by Tom Fettke

50

Honor and Praise

Words and Music by
TWILA PARIS
Arranged by Camp Kirkland
Duet arrangement by Tom Fettke

Warmly, with movement ♩ = ca. 135

1st time: Both voices unison melody
2nd time: Divisi - High voice sing countermelody

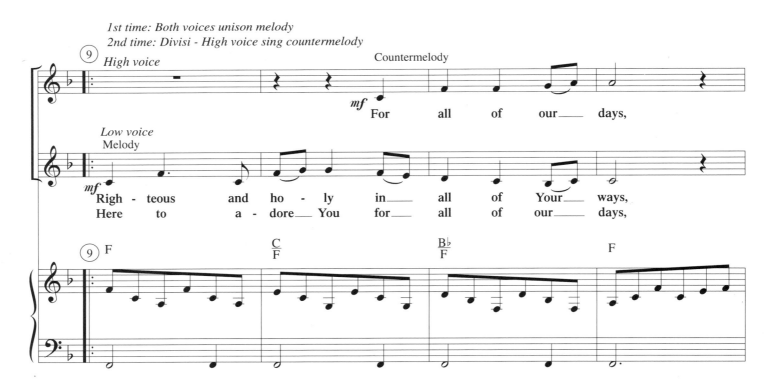

High voice
Countermelody
mf For all of our____ days,

Low voice
Melody
mf Righ - teous and ho - ly in____ all of Your____ ways,
Here to a - dore____ You for____ all of our____ days,

The Weight of the Cross

Words and Music by
CHRISTOPHER MACHEN
*Arranged by Camp Kirkland
and Tom Fettke*

Heal Our Land

with
America, the Beautiful

Words and Music by
TOM and ROBIN BROOKS
Arranged by Tom Fettke

68

*"America, the Beautiful" (Bible, Bates/Ward)

Lyrics:

heal our bro - ken land. _____ O

beau - ti - ful for men of faith Who found - ed this great land; Pro -

claimed for us, "In God we trust," And held to God's strong hand. A -

mer - i - ca! A - mer - i - ca! God shed His grace on thee Till

He Came to Me

with

He Giveth More Grace

Words and Music by
SQUIRE E. PARSONS, JR.
Arranged by Tom Fettke

73

74

love I now a - bide.   His

43 *"He Giveth More Grace" (Flint/Mitchell)

love has no lim - it; His grace has no mea - sure; His

47

pow'r has no bound - a - ry known un - to man.

52 a tempo   me.

He came to me,   He came to me, He came to

Antiphonal Praise
with
How Great Is He

Arranged by Tom Fettke

With adoration ♩ = ca. 80

*"How Great Is He" (Johnson-Fettke)

82

Jesus Christ Is the Lord of All

Words and Music by
DAN WHITTEMORE
Arranged by Camp Kirkland
and Tom Fettke

1. Of pres-i-dents, princ-es, rul-ers and Kings, who of all____ shall reign su-preme?____

We Are Waiting on You

Words and Music by
KIM NOBLITT and CHRIS SPRINGER
Arranged by Tom Fettke

People Need the Lord

Words and Music by
GREG NELSON and PHILL McHUGH
Arranged by Tom Fettke

15 *Both voices unison*

On they go   through pri - vate pain,   Liv-ing fear   to   fear;

19   *rit.*

Laugh-ter hides   their si - lent cries   on-ly Je-sus   hears.

23 *High voice*
a tempo
mp

Peo - ple need   the Lord,____   Peo-ple need   the Lord;____

Low voice
mp

Peo - ple need__ the Lord,____   Peo-ple need   the Lord;____

95

We are called to take His light To a world where wrong seems right;_____

What could be too great a cost For shar-ing life with one who's lost?

In Christ Alone

Words and Music by
SHAWN CRAIG and DON KOCH
Arranged by Tom Fettke

100

I Stand Here Forgiven

Words and Music by
GREG NELSON and PHIL McHUGH
Arranged by Tom Fettke

Verse 1: Solo or both voices unison
Verse 2: Both voices unison

1. I am God's child, I stand here for-giv-en, My sins have been cast in the depths of the sea.
2. I have good news, your sins are for-giv-en, They're far-ther a-way than the east is from west.

2nd time: ladies unison

I have been washed in the stream of sal-va-tion, And I am free.
Come now and bathe in God's stream of sal-va-tion, And know His

rest.

Here We Stand

KEN BIBLE

TOM FETTKE
Arranged by Tom Fettke

112

Lord of All

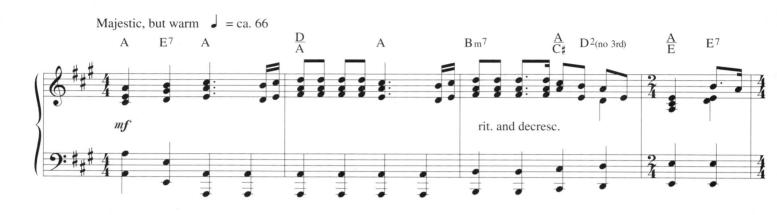

Words and Music by
PHILL McHUGH
Arranged by Tom Fettke

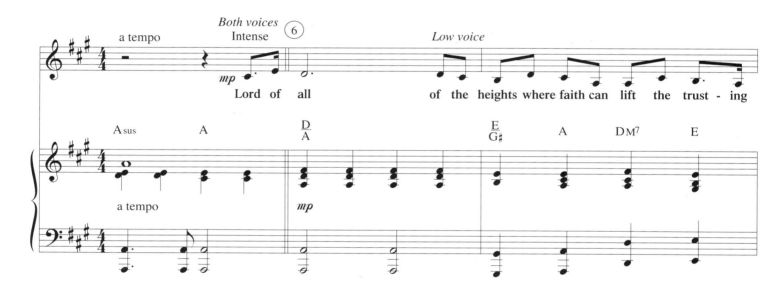

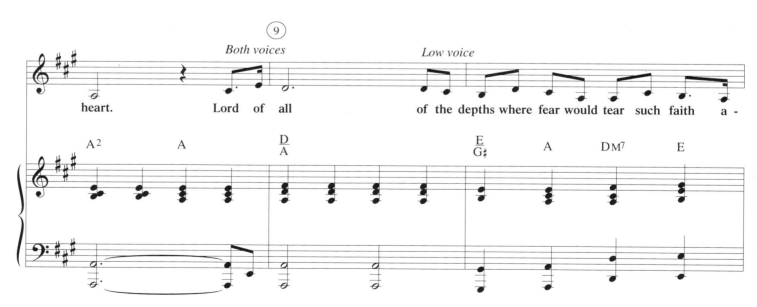

116

pow - er not to sin;___ You have al - ways been and al - ways will be   Lord of___ all.

rit. and decresc.

a tempo   *Both voices*   ㉜   *Low voice*

Lord of all   of a peace that we can draw from ev - ery

Both voices   ㉟   *Low voice*

breath.   Lord of all   of pro - vi - sion for each need in life and

118

It's Still the Cross

Words and Music by
NILES BOROP, MIKE HARLAND,
LUKE GARRETT and BUDDY MULLINS
Arranged by Camp Kirkland
Duet arrangement by Tom Fettke

Tenderly ♩ = ca. 56

*Solo or both voices unison

1. It's not con-ser-va-tive___ or lib-er-al, how-ev-er they're de-fined; It's not a-
strat-e-gize___ and im-ple-ment our stanc-es and___ de-crees; We can con-

bout in-ter-pre-ta-tions, or the judg-ments of the mind.___ It's the
trol our in-sti-tu-tions, ap-prove and grant de-grees.___ But the

* It would be most effective if the two voices sing alternate verses or phrases.

122

Shine on Us

Words and Music by
MICHAEL W. SMITH
and DEBORAH SMITH
Arranged by Bruce Greer
Duet arrangement by Tom Fettke

(to pg. 123, ms. 7)

Midnight Cry

Words and Music by
GREG DAY and CHUCK DAY
Arranged by Tom Fettke